PIANO • VOCAL • GUITAR

THE
GAVIN DEGRAW
SHEET MUSIC COLLECTION

Produced by
Alfred Music Publishing Co., Inc.
P.O. Box 10003
Van Nuys, CA 91410-0003
alfred.com

Printed in USA.

ISBN-10: 0-7390-8659-6
ISBN-13: 978-0-7390-8659-9

Cover photo © The Picture Group

Album art: *Chariot* © 2003 J Records • *Gavin DeGraw* © 2008 J Records • *Free* © 2009 J Records • *Sweeter* © 2011 RCA Records

 Alfred Cares. Contents printed on 100% recycled paper.

CONTENTS

FOLLOW THROUGH

Words and Music by
GAVIN DeGRAW

Moderately ♩ = 88

1. Oh, this is the start of some-thing good.
2. These reel-ing e-mo - tions, they just keep me a - live,

Don't you a - gree? I have-n't felt like
they keep me in tune. Oh, look what I'm hold -

this in so man - y moons. You know what I mean?
ing here in my fire. This is for you.

6

for you to stick_ a-round. I'll see you ev-'ry day,_

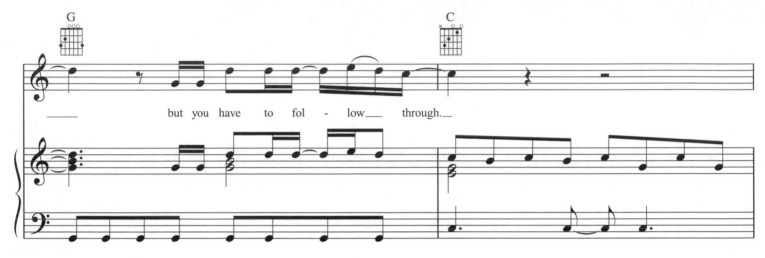

but you have to fol-low_ through._

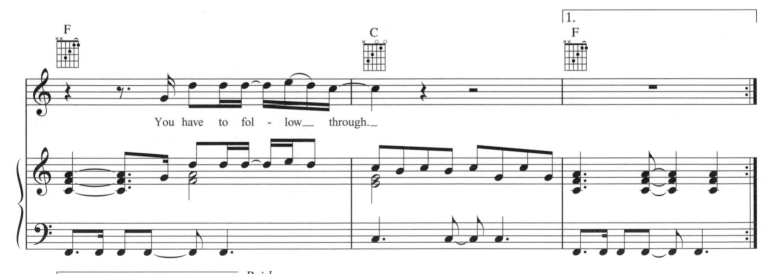

You have to fol-low_ through._

1.

2.

Bridge:

The words you say_ to me__ are un-like an-y-thing_

that's ev - er been said.　　　Oh, and what you do__ to me__

is un - like an - y - thing__ that's ev - er been.__　　Am I too

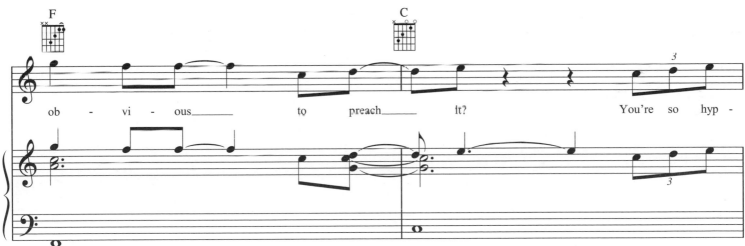

ob - vi - ous__ to preach__ it?　　You're so hyp -

not - ic on__ my heart.__

8

Chorus:

CHARIOT

Words and Music by
GAVIN DeGRAW

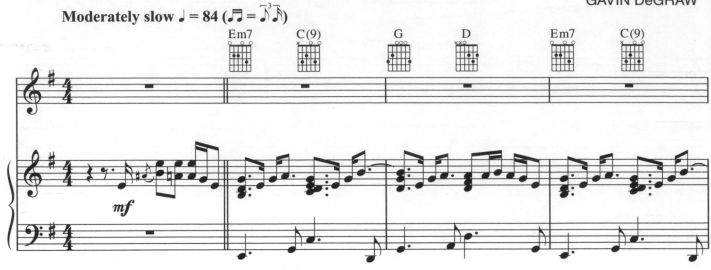

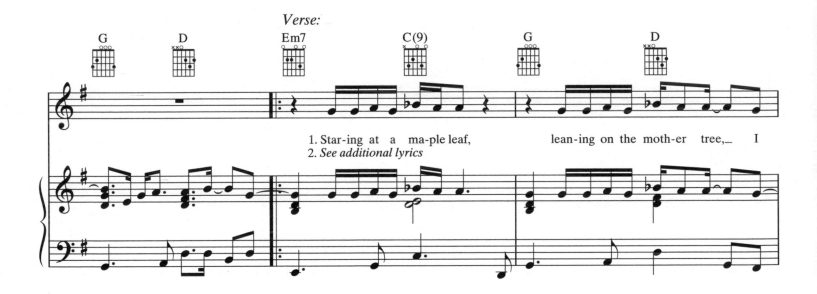

Verse:

1. Star-ing at a ma-ple leaf, lean-ing on the moth-er tree,__ I
2. *See additional lyrics*

said to my-self, we've all lost touch.__ Your fa-v'rite fruit__

Chariot - 5 - 1

D.S. 𝄋 *al Coda*

Verse 2:
Remember seeking moon's rebirth?
Rains made mirrors of the earth.
The sun was just yellow energy.
There is a living promise land,
Even over fields of sand.
Seasons fill my mind and cover me.
Bring it back.
More than a memory.
(To Chorus:)

I DON'T WANT TO BE

Words and Music by
GAVIN DeGRAW

Verse:

1. I don't need to be an-y-thing oth-er than a pris-on guard's son.
2. I'm sur-round-ed by li-ars ev-'ry-where I turn.

I Don't Want to Be - 5 - 1

Bridge:

Can I have ev - 'ry-one's at - ten-tion, please?_

(Spoken:) If you're not like this and that, you're gonna have to leave.

I came from the moun - tain, the crust of cre - a - tion.

D.S. %. al Coda

My whole sit - u - a - tion made from clay to stone, and now I'm tell - in' ev - 'ry-bod - y.

JUST FRIENDS

Words and Music by
GAVIN DeGRAW

22

MORE THAN ANYONE

Words and Music by
GAVIN DeGRAW

Slow ballad ♩ = 63
Verse:

(Play cue notes second time only)

1. You need a friend;___ I'll be a-round.___
2. Look in my eyes;___ what do you see?___

Don't let this end be-fore I see you a-gain.
Not just the col-or; look in-side___ of me.

What can I say___ to con-vince___ you to change___ your mind___
Tell me all___ you need,___ and I___ will try;

More Than Anyone - 3 - 1

CHEATED ON ME

Words and Music by
GAVIN DeGRAW

And it is-n't hard to be-lieve___ I think you cheat-ed on___ me.

I think she cheat-ed on___ me.___

Bridge:

___ I said I've had this sense___ be-fore,_____ but I left an o-pen door___

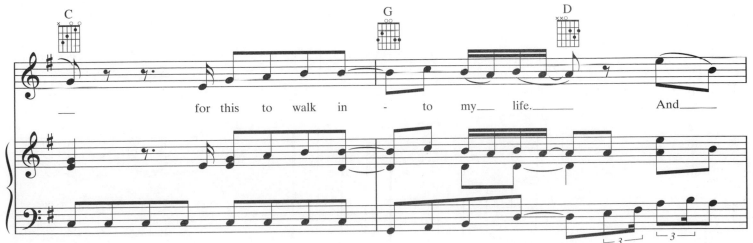

___ for this to walk in-to my___ life._____ And_____

IN LOVE WITH A GIRL

Words and Music by
GAVIN DeGRAW

I HAVE YOU TO THANK

Words and Music by
GAVIN DeGRAW

1. When-ev-er I see___ you, I___ need more___ and I want___

___ you to stay___ 'til the end.___ One look at that smile___ and I'm___ all___ yours._

40

SHE HOLDS A KEY

Words and Music by
GAVIN DeGRAW

She Holds a Key - 5 - 1

46

Chorus:

She holds a key____ tight in her hand.___ Clutch - ing his

neck, she is break - ing the man._____ Lis - ten, you sin - ner, I'm sin - ning too.___

____ Just wait un - til the dark - ness falls,___ so I can sin with you.___

Verse 2:
You've run through the whole gamut of gameplay,
The head-trip parade.
Without any experience,
You've become curious prey.
So, change your position.
This decision you're making is digging a hole,
Oh, and where you're headed only heaven knows.
(To Chorus:)

WE BELONG TOGETHER

Words and Music by
GAVIN DeGRAW

We be-long to-geth - er,___ like the o - pen

seas and shores,_ wed-ded by the plan-et floors._

Verse 1:

1. The ham-mer may strike

me dead on the ground,_____

a nail to my hand,   a cross on this crown.

But we're done__ if we're__ un - done,__

____ fin - ished if____ we__ are__ in - com - plete._____

Verse 2:

2. What good is a life

with no one to share   the light of the moon,_____

_____   mmm, the hon-or of a   swear?__

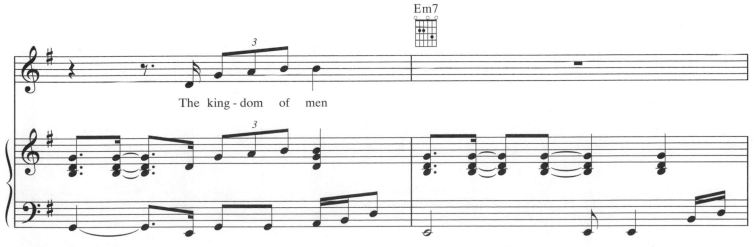

The king-dom of men

58

DANCING SHOES

Words and Music by
GAVIN DeGRAW

Moderately, with movement ♩ = 126

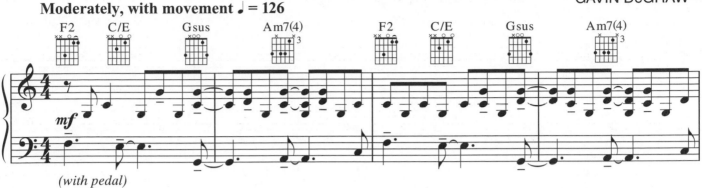

(with pedal)

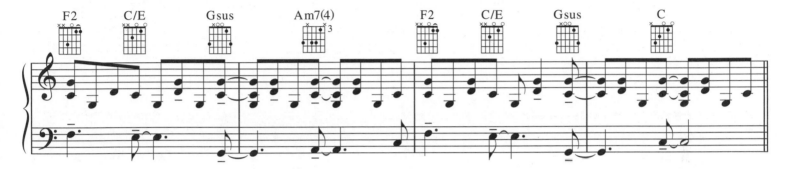

Verses 1 & 2:

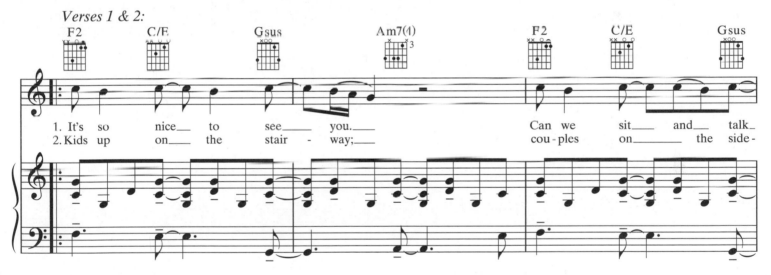

1. It's so nice to see you. Can we sit and talk
2. Kids up on the stair - way; cou - ples on the side -

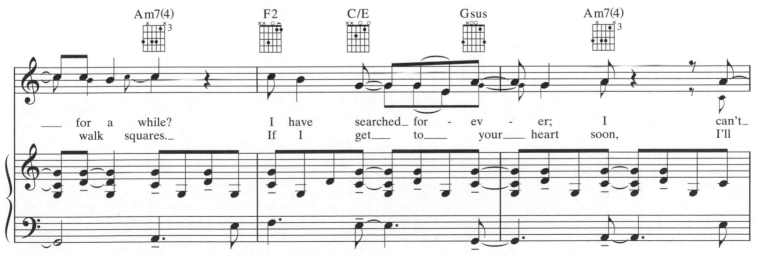

for a while? I have searched for - ev - er; I can't
walk squares. If I get to your heart soon, I'll

64

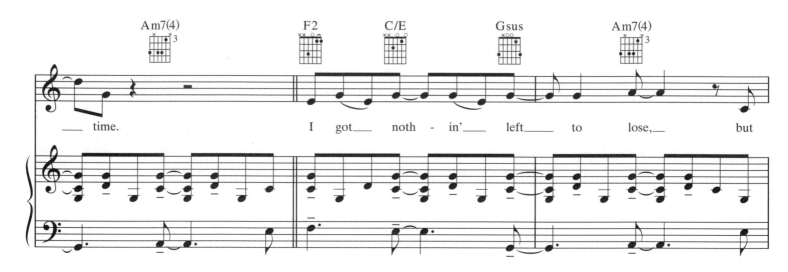

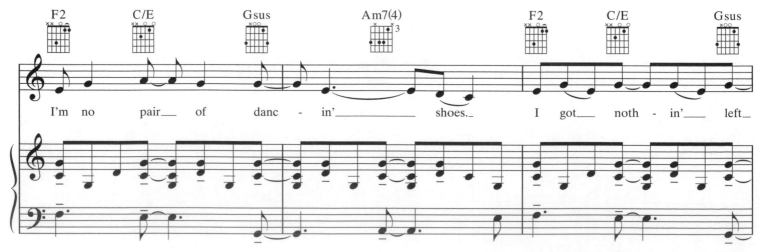

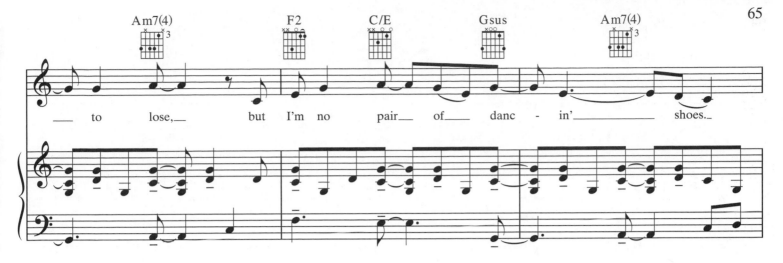

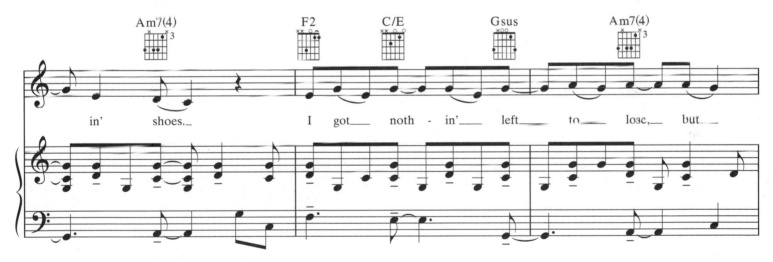

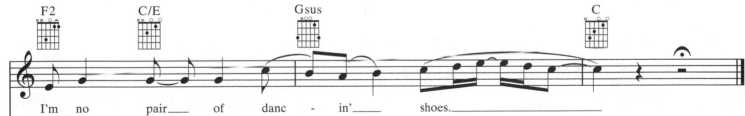

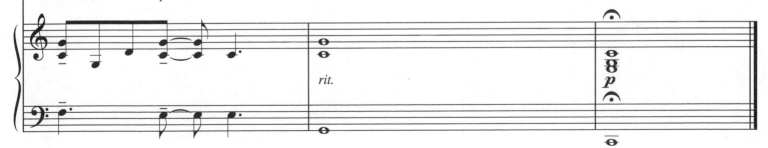

FREE

Words and Music by
GAVIN DeGRAW

Slow groove ♩ = 72   *Verse 1:*

Free - 8 - 1

Free - 8 - 2

me. I'll give you ev - 'ry - thing___ that you would ev - er

need. Ooh,_____

ooh,_____ ooh._____

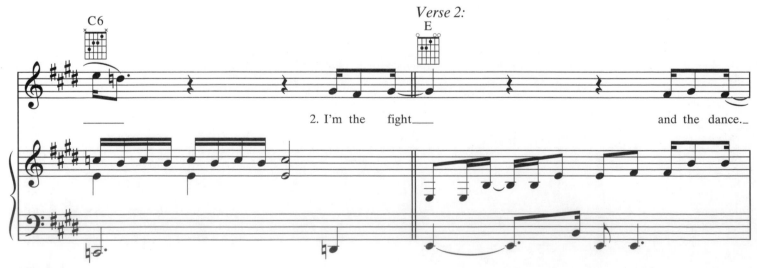

_____ 2. I'm the fight___ and the dance._

I__ am heart - break__ and__ ro - mance,

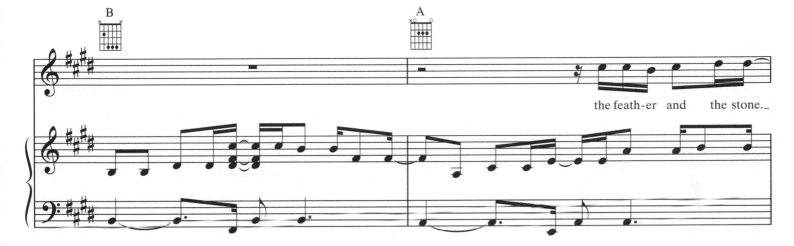

the feath-er and the stone.__

I feel crowd - ed and a lonc.__

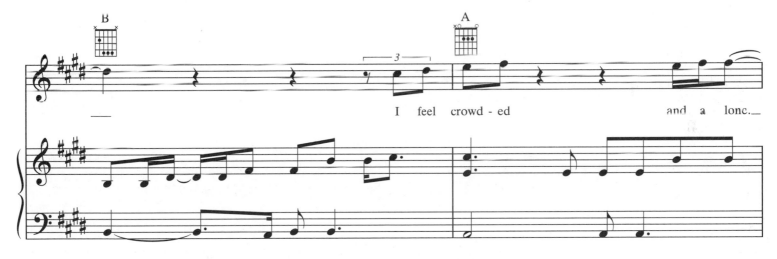

___ And I wan-na be free,__ wind in my

Chorus:

mf

while,_____ I wan-na sit back__ and en - joy___ the view._

___ I'm feel-in' my sens - es,_____ but,

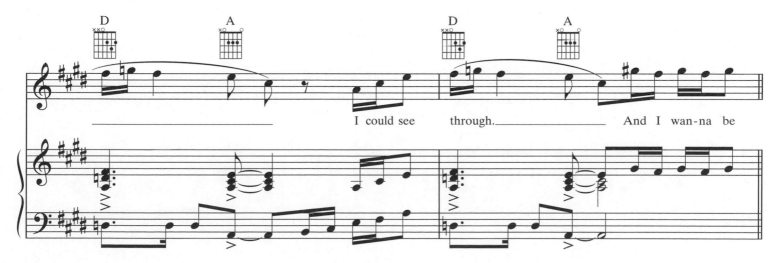

wom-an, my___ life has been sur-round-ed by__ fenc-es, but I found some that I could see through,_

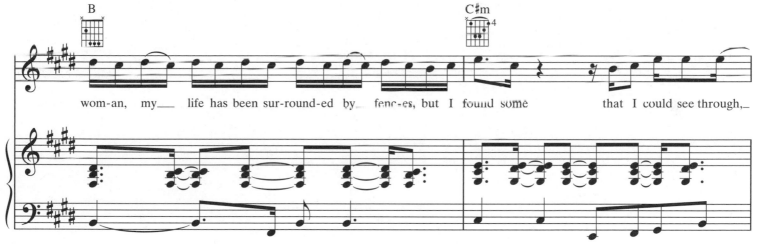

_____ I could see through._____ And I wan-na be

Chorus:

ev - 'ry-thing that you_____ would ev - er need,_____

ev - 'ry-thing that you would ev - er_____ need._____

___ (1st time only; lead vocal ad lib. repeat and fade)

Repeat ad lib. and fade

SWEETER

Words and Music by
GAVIN DeGRAW and RYAN TEDDER

Verse 1 (sing 1st time only):

1. You, you don't know how luck-y you are,

Verse 2 (sing 2nd time only):

2. You went to school and found out you're dumb.

hang-ing with that girl on your arm. But soon e-nough, I'm tak-ing my shot.

May-be you just had too much fun, fell in love and think it's the one.

Sweeter - 5 - 1

Verse 3:

3. I'm - ma rec - om - mend_ you take that bod - y to the oth - er end.__ I real - ly like you, but I can't be friends,_ not_ with these hands_____ of mine._____

sim.

(Drums only)

NOT OVER YOU

Words and Music by
GAVIN DeGRAW and RYAN TEDDER

Not Over You - 9 - 1

Verse 2:

2. Damn, damn, girl, you do it well. And I thought you were in - no - cent. Took this heart and put in through hell, but still, you're mag - nif - i - cent. I, I'm a boo - mer - ang. Does - n't mat - ter how you throw me,

RUN EVERY TIME

Words and Music by
GAVIN DeGRAW and ANDREW FRAMPTON

Run Every Time - 6 - 1

Chorus:

SOLDIER

Words and Music by
GAVIN DeGRAW

Chorus:

I'll get it if you need it. I'll search if you {don't}{can't} see it.

You're thirst-y, I'll be rain. You get hurt, I'll take your pain.

I know, you don't be-lieve it. But I said it and I still mean it,

when you heard what I told you. When you get wor-ried, I'll be your sol - dier.

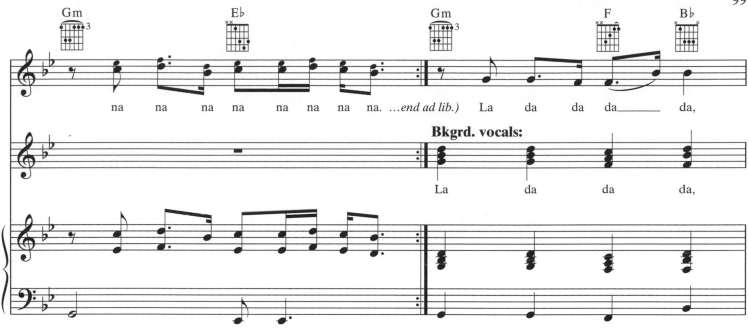

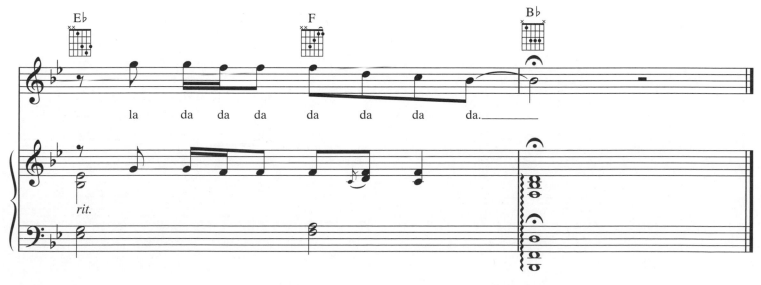

YOU KNOW WHERE I'M AT

Words and Music by
GAVIN DeGRAW

SPELL IT OUT

Words and Music by
GAVIN DeGRAW and ANDREW FRAMPTON

Slowly ♩ = 76
Verse:

1. With my eyes wide o - pen__ and with words un - spo - ken,__
2. Oh, when I first met you,__ there were things I'd been through__

(with pedal)

__ I still un - der - stand.__
__ that I would nev - er tell.__

And I'm read - ing your mind,__ us - ing ev - er - y out - line__
But it was al - most as if__ you al - read - y knew my lan - guage,__

Spell It Out - 5 - 1

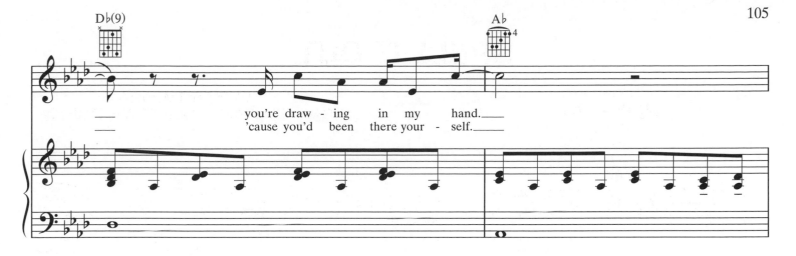

you're draw - ing in my hand.___
'cause you'd been there your - self.___

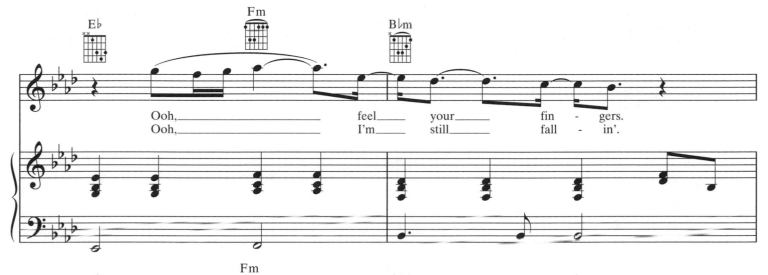

Ooh,_____ feel___ your_____ fin - gers.
Ooh,_____ I'm___ still_____ fall - in'.

Ooh,_____ I'm___ in way___ too deep___ to }wake_
Ooh,_____ don't___ make me___ re - turn___ and}

𝄋 *Chorus:*

___ up,_____ step___ out.____ 'Cause I'm real -